CONTENTS

PIVOT Magazine

Founder and President
Jason Miller
jason@strategicadvisorboard.com

Editor-in-Chief
Chris O'Byrne
chris@jetlaunch.net

Design
JETLAUNCH.net

Advertising
Chris O'Byrne
chris@jetlaunch.net

Webmaster
Joel Phillips
joel@proshark.com

Editor
Laura West
laura@jetlaunch.net

Cover Design
Debbie O'Byrne

FROM THE EDITOR

This is the second of two special editions highlighting some of the incredible members who are part of The Bellwether Alliance.

Since being introduced to The Bellwether Alliance and subsequently interviewing several members (including the Viceroy), I've been deeply impressed by the level of character and servant leadership displayed.

Instead of giving each article in this magazine a title, we chose to simply use the name of the Bellwether member highlighted.

As you'll see as you read through the articles, the breadth of experience of Bellwether members is vast. Yet, each one follows the principles and credo and strives to grow and serve.

You can learn more about The Bellwether Alliance at thebellwetheralliance.com.

FROM THE DESK OF THE PRESIDENT

Jason Miller

Companies grow and scale because they put in the work. The key to scaling any company is taking it through the proper procedures that allow it to scale. You have to create and optimize a process that works for you, your customers, and your niche. For my company, it starts with acquisition and ends with making every customer our biggest cheerleader.

Many young or even seasoned business owners forget one of these steps, or they have a bottleneck in the system somewhere. The secret sauce really is not a secret. You scale a company by optimizing the following steps.

- Acquisition process
- Sales process
- Onboarding process
- Support process
- Communication process
- Fulfillment process

- Referral process
- Internal process and procedure to support the above customer pipeline

Then the next conversation becomes a "growth" conversation. Many business owners think they are one and the same. In reality, growth and scale are two sides of the business working in parallel. Growth is people and process, and scale is the monetary side of the business. These areas must run in parallel so there is no imbalance in the infrastructure.

I think some of the most meaningful moments are those small wins. You see the first result when you get started or you get your first customer. For our company, a very meaningful moment just came this year. I woke up and was notified by our public relations team that *Forbes Magazine* had just released a feature on our company. It's not always about money; business is about being proud to serve your community and create meaningful footprints.

As far as obstacles go, there are hundreds of them. I call them landmines because we often have no idea that they are coming. It could be as simple as a part of your technology has failed, and you have no idea why your sales stopped all of a sudden. Tactical task management is an everyday obstacle in business. You have to manage your business from the CEO seat, not the seat of the operations manager. Learn to shed tactical tasks so you can do your job effectively.

I don't believe in mistakes; I believe in lessons. Every business owner out there learns lessons, both good and bad. I have learned a share of my own while creating multiple companies. We drop the ball on a customer follow-up, and now it creates issues or refunds. If you are reading this as a business owner, you already know the buckets full of issues that come up every day.

One of the key things I think is far overlooked by business owners is self-guided leadership. As a leader of an organization, you have to balance your own plate before you can try to balance those in your C-suite or staff sections. You have to align your business plan with your life plan so you have the proper synergy between your home and work life. If you can't lead yourself effectively, then how can you possibly expect to lead others?

In 2016, I had a vision of creating a company that could help small businesses grow and thrive. I didn't want to disable them with fees before we even got started, and I also wanted businesses to keep the revenue they had already generated on their own. But I wanted to help businesses grow and take a larger piece of the marketplace. My vision was to be the opposite of the huge consulting firms and create custom solutions that resulted in Rapid Revenue for small businesses. We wouldn't get paid unless we helped create a result. Most said I was crazy and that it would never work. I continued the course, and we have helped hundreds of companies shift and pivot and grow.

The Strategic Advisor Board was forged out of the sheer desire to be different, to go left when everyone else was going right. To disrupt the market and shift the "consulting model" into a more streamlined company that helps small businesses get results. The focus is on the business, the immediate needs of the business in its stage of development, and the long-term strategy to create robust growth within the company. I surround myself with experts in other areas of business so we can provide the best solutions for our clients. The best part is that we have a trusted network of business service providers under the Strategic Advisory Board (SAB) umbrella to fulfill the steps in the strategy. The SAB is your business growth authority and solutions resource center.

Our reason is very simple. We have all been through the yo-yo of business ownership. My design allows us to help business owners finally put down the yo-yo and surround themselves with ten professional working CEOs who have been there and done that. Who has gone through the challenges of ownership and come out on the other side successfully?

The Strategic Advisor Board (SAB) is one of a kind in the marketplace. Ten CEOs in the SAB are powerful leaders in their own businesses, brought together under one umbrella to provide the best growth strategy and path for small businesses. The collective experience in the SAB established their business growth model in many different interactions with their clients. Not only does the SAB identify a comprehensive growth strategy for businesses, but we also partner with the business owners to execute the strategy

through short-term strategy and long-term goals. The SAB is focused on custom solutions and strong relationships.

The power of the SAB is in the diversity in the background and approach within the board. The differing backgrounds of the board members enable the strategies to be articulated for businesses at any stage, but in particular, those businesses that have grown and are sustainable and ready to begin reaching a larger audience, engaging more clients in their business, and are ready to create additional streams of revenue in their business. An all-inclusive strategy map adjusts with the needs of each business to grow and scale the movement of the marketplace. The additional power of the SAB comes from the network of trusted partners to help businesses execute the strategy. With over 100 referral partners in the SAB, the guesswork is taken out of the planning and how to implement the solutions.

Our Rapid Revenue and Results model acts like a model airplane. There is your vision of the completed product, a clearly articulated, step-by-step process to help you achieve that vision, all of the necessary pieces of the model, the tools needed to put together the pieces, and the glue that holds everything together to finally complete the product.

The SAB acts in a similar way. The SAB creates a unique vision in our partnership with the affiliated business. That framework serves as the guiding path for a business to follow. Then the step-by-step process to generate quick revenue to pay for their next stage of growth. Next, we implement the strategies to help achieve that vision. We use our trusted toolbox/network of trusted service providers to provide the necessary connections to implement the strategies. The glue is the consistent interaction with the SAB board members in our partnership to ensure we are moving your business to the next level. We copilot the strategies with you to adapt to the changing conditions in the marketplace and ensure the business's success.

The long-term strategy architecture serves as the roadmap for the business that focuses on a lasting foundation and community. We explore strategies of how to best engage your ideal client, create a consistent base of referral partners, explore multiple revenue streams in your business, and help create your exit strategy for when you are ready to depart the business.

Reputation is everything, and you can build it over a lifetime and ruin it in less than thirty seconds. We have gone to great lengths to create quality services for our clients. This, in turn, has gotten us noticed on the national media stage multiple times to share our story. If you focus on giving more value than you promised as a business, then your clients will award you for it. They will give you great testimonials that build your credibility on platforms such as Google My Business and BBB. These are trusted platforms where your customers can leave feedback. Provide great service, and the rest will fall into place!

The best way you can grow your client base is just to be yourself. Be real, be genuine, and don't run a company with smoke and mirrors. If you are a small company, it's okay to be a small company or, as I call it, a "little giant." Own that and embrace that as you grow through the business lifecycle. I see so many pop-up firms that want to look like a giant when, in reality, they are not. This leads to hard lessons and can ultimately have a very negative effect on a business as it will always affect the fulfillment process. Be who you are, embrace the shoes you currently fill, and grow from there.

CAROL T. CARPENTER

MotoVixens is more than a brand; it is my purpose and my passion. Part of that purpose is not just bringing more women and young riders into motorcycling but elevating and preserving the sport for many generations to come. Being very naïve when I first entered the industry, I said some choice words that raised eyebrows and got me laughed at. I stated, "Women are the future of this sport." It's obviously a male-dominated industry, and of course, they laughed at me like I was a joke.

Fast forward, eight years later, one of the premier crew chiefs in the nation was doing a presentation at an orientation meeting for new racers. I remember him standing at the front of the room, looking directly at me, saying, "Women are the future of the sport." And just like that, I finally got validation.

It took me eight years to get that validation, and it took having a well-respected man in the industry to say that for people to take it seriously. I found it really disheartening that people couldn't necessarily see the goal, or the trends of their industry, and for whatever reason, I could. But at the time, I was laughed at. I was a joke. And now looking back, I'm like, "Nah, I was just ahead of my time."

It takes time for people to start to change their minds, to change the paradigm, but it's been clear for a while that the motorcycle industry has been geared towards males because it is mostly men who are involved in the sport. Even gear and apparel companies and the motorcycles themselves are all geared towards men. But if you look at the spending trends within the industry, women riders are strong purchasers, they buy things, and they buy in multiples. In fact, they buy even for their spouses, significant others, and friends. Men only buy one at a time, and they'll wear the crap out of it. Women will buy multiples; we love choices.

I have an entire rack in my hanger that is just motorcycle gear from textiles to leathers to race suits—you name it. It's an entire garment rack. Men may have one race suit, maybe two, so they have a backup. But when a woman spends, she spends! So wouldn't you agree you're better off marketing toward a woman than a man? And by the way, if you have a guy that rides, who do you think buys for that man? Typically, a woman.

Women really are the future of the sport. People are just slow to accept it. Since I started over ten years ago, I think there were maybe three women that would show up at a track day. So, maybe three women to every two hundred men. Now, I see the ratios are far greater. I see at least a dozen, if not more, each track day and the numbers continue to grow.

I think it comes down to making the sport more mainstream. People see motorcycling as a dangerous sport, but just like anything else, it's not dangerous if you get an education. I personally think skiing is way more dangerous, and I did that too. I often think,

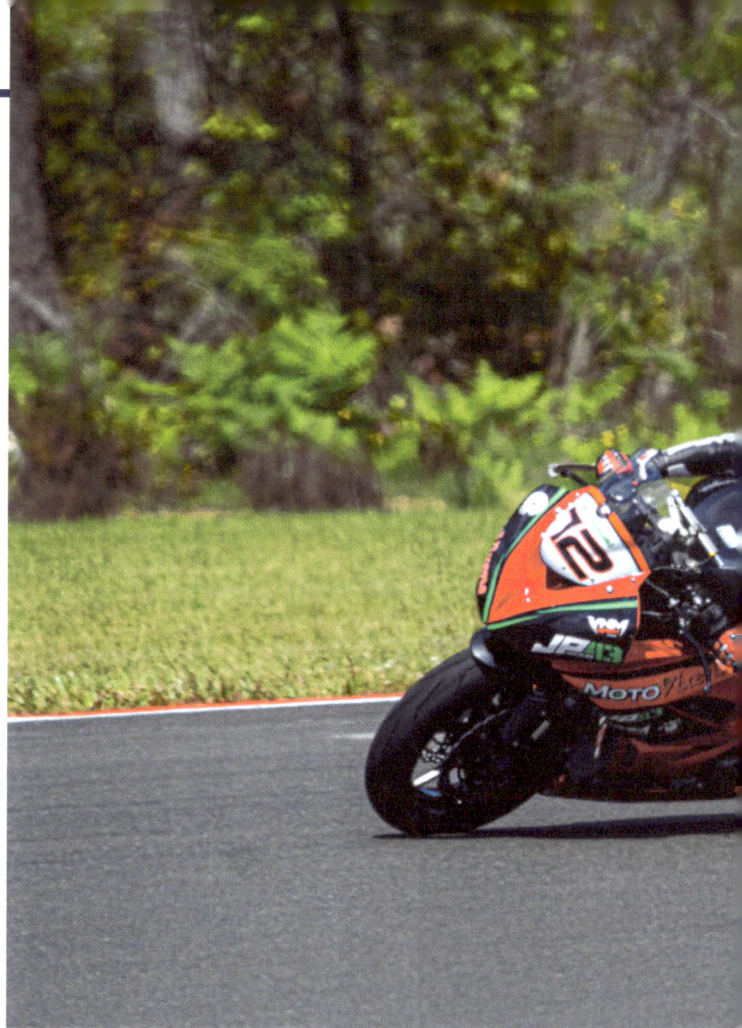

You think motorcycling is dangerous? Shoot. I mean, I've been taken out sideways, hit by people, and flipped because they can't control themselves down a hill. I think I've incurred worse injuries skiing than I ever have riding a motorcycle.

I road race and I also street ride, the same fundamentals apply to both. Riding on track makes you a better rider on the street because you build your skillset, get confident and you become more aware. In the fall and winter we cross-train with dirt biking and flat tracking to stay, not only in shape, but keep improving. You must become very comfortable with your bike sliding underneath you when you are on the track, and the only way to get that kind of feeling is to

do some flat tracking and some dirt biking. Training in the off-season is vital.

On the street, I ride with the notion that I am invisible because, most of the time, I feel like I am. I never assume that anybody can see me or hear me. I have a Ducati that I ride on the street, and it has a *really* loud exhaust. It has a set of Yoshimura racing pipes. They are freaking loud. And you would think, just like a Harley, people would hear them. But the truth is, if someone isn't paying attention, they're not paying attention. They're on their phones. They're talking to their kids. They have music playing in their car. There are so many distractions.

In fact, I was once riding in the carpool lane (as a motorcyclist, you can ride the carpool lanes), and there was a lady who clearly was distracted in the car next to me (she was in the fast lane). I think she had a child in the back seat. She started to veer into the carpool lane. She didn't see me, and I had to move out of her way. I went all the way over toward the cement center divider. I was on a highway! So, I'm just sitting there thinking, *You've got to be kidding me.* The only thing that we have as a saving grace as a motorcyclist is speed. So, in order to get away from her, I accelerated really quickly to get out of the way because if I hadn't, and I froze, she would've rammed me into that cement center divider. A car is a cage. We are exposed, we don't get a second chance, we don't have any other protection than the gear we wear, and we are the ones who lose. Let's remember that riders are not just guys that are fathers, husbands, brothers, friends, but also women that are mothers, wives, sisters…we share those roads with you. Please watch out for us.

Most people don't think about the possible outcome of being distracted. They are driving on four wheels and surrounded by metal. If something minor happens, it's just an insurance claim. We aren't offered the same luxury. A mistake on our part or due to another person can be life changing. While what happens to motorcyclists in these events can be tragic, it could also have serious repercussions for you as a driver, as well. On the extreme, you could even be put in jail for a fatality. People aren't thinking; they're just so distracted, preoccupied, stressed, sleep deprived, etc. As a fellow rider, I always advise them to ride like they're invisible. It keeps us present and focused and helps us avoid potential issues.

On the racetrack, we have a saying, "It's not about if you're going to crash, it's when." It's not to scare people, but eventually, you are going to push the limits and possibly push the limits too far, and you're going to crash, which is why we are outfitted in the best gear possible. We wear leather suits because it is a second skin. We have great protective helmets these days. The technology is incredible. The helmets are designed to be tight because if you have a helmet that's one size too big for your head, you might as well not be wearing a helmet at all. You're making scrambled eggs, essentially. We wear this protective gear to save our skin and our noggins, which is very important for the functioning of the rest of our bodies.

I never thought that I could manage two crashes into one, but I did! So, we have "high sides" and "low sides". High sides are when your bike flicks you off like a booger and low sides are when your bike ends up sliding on one side. Low sides don't tend to be violent or serious crashes, and you usually get slowed down by gravel, asphalt, grass, or sand before you come to a stop.

So, I was coming up a hill in Shelton, specifically turn three, which is lovingly called "The Collector" for good reason: It collects a lot of bikes (and riders). That corner has a camber, and back then, before the re-asphalting, there was a slight lip. I've ridden it a million times. I thought that I was lucky because I hadn't had a get-off on that one yet, but that was my day.

That was my day, for sure. I came into turn three, and either I took it wrong, the tires were cold, or I was too quick on the throttle. Who knows what it was, but I found myself low siding. As I started to slide into a low side, to my surprise, my tires caught the curbing. Next thing I realize is my bike is headed in one direction and I'm in the air like superwoman, flying from one side of the track and landing in the middle of the track with riders heading up the hill! I call that crash my twofer. What it taught me was, even though I was in the midst of all this, to remain calm and relax. I walked away unscathed, and my bike did remarkably well, also.

Most people are scared to hear about crashes, but it really isn't as bad as people

make it out to be. I survived, so have most of those who have crashed before me. We can survive these crashes; it just requires remaining calm and having some knowledge of what to do when it happens. It's usually when you panic and freeze that bad things can happen. If you can relax into it, you have a much greater chance of surviving. We talk a lot about it because it does happen so fast. Sometimes, you don't even have time to respond. And there've been instances of guys coming back and saying, "Oh my God, I was in the crash. And then suddenly, I saw what looked like my feet. Somebody had my boots, and I couldn't figure out why somebody had my boots." (That was them realizing that they're actually flying through the air.)

There are some funny stories that come from crashes, but almost everybody survives. You've got bumps and bruises, maybe even have scrapes and cuts—and let's face it, your ego and confidence takes a hit, also—but you have to get back on that bike. And the truth is, for many of us, if we are physically able, we *will* get right back on because we need to fight that fear immediately. If it has time to fester, it makes us question our abilities and that inner chatter only increases.

I was a late bloomer when I got into motorcycle riding. I was going through a divorce, and I was learning to ride through the MSF Course. I sucked. I mean, I seriously sucked, and I don't like to suck at anything. So, once I got my endorsement, I started going to track schools, riding much more regularly, and trying to overcome that fear. I don't like being afraid, I prefer to face it straight on. It's like with guns. People are afraid of guns, but I'm like, *Really, you're afraid of guns? Shit, let's go shoot.* I don't run away, and I don't let it consume me, I use it to fuel my desire to crush those fears. I'd rather challenge things and face them than run away and be afraid. I never want to be afraid of anything.

That's how my experience with motorcycling started. I was like, *Okay, I suck. I don't want to suck. So, I'm going to get better.* I became good enough to instruct for other organizations, and I was invited to do that as well. During those track days, I heard what clients liked and disliked and relayed that feedback to the organizers. They didn't care nor did they see the information as valuable. It became harder and harder to work for these organizations, so I took the feedback and started doing things my way. Which leads me to today, celebrating ten years in business.

I was blessed with an opportunity to write a book that has become a bestseller (available on Amazon), *The Elegant Disruptor*. Earlier this year, I was invited to do a TEDx talk, which you can find on YouTube. I also cohost on a podcast with Travis Johnson called the *Titan Evolution Podcast*, plus I have a reality show, am an executive producer of an upcoming film, have a signature line of products, and am the managing partner of Iron Dog Media. For details visit *irondog.media*.

I am working on a joint venture with some-one who also wants to focus on working with women entrepreneurs. We want to give women a platform on which to gain interest for their companies. If they have products or services they are launching, we want to help them succeed Many of us started out in male-dominated industries and felt we didn't have the opportunities we wish we would have had firsthand, so we want to create that platform for them.

Overall, my goal is simply to help people. I want to know I made a really big positive impact in this world. That's my end goal—to

make sure I've touched a lot of lives in a very positive manner and helped many, many people along the way.

When I was starting out, my family wanted me to be a doctor. I think maybe feeling that pressure all those years to be a doctor had me thinking about why that appealed to me. I care. It's ingrained in me, and maybe the reason I do what I do. I care about people. I want to make sure to find ways and to give them avenues to succeed. When they succeed, we all succeed. Being a mentor is the ultimate way of giving back, watching others become better versions of themselves and offering their unique gifts to society. We each have our own contributions we can make to make a larger positive impact in the world, and it is our responsibility to leave it better than when we entered into it.

I think too many people use logic to make decisions. I say use your intuition. I've learned to trust mine, and if I hadn't used my intuition to go into motorcycling, I wouldn't be here today in the same capacity. I most certainly was never into motorcycles growing up, so to be where I am is surprising. My best advice is to listen to that voice inside because sometimes your mind is so busy that you're not paying attention anymore. If you see signs or if there is a repetitive feeling or dream, pay attention, it could end up being your calling. Have courage to take the road less traveled. Why be afraid? Go for it! Who knows what could happen!

DAN VEGA

I grew up in Los Angeles and came from a middle-class and somewhat humble beginning. My mother was a teacher's aide, and my father was a salesman. I grew up in a survival mindset, such as which bills to pay and which ones to delay.

I also have a condition called synesthesia, which has drawbacks. It's like a form of autism and where your five senses get crossed. Some people can smell color or see music. But for me, I've always had a very high understanding of mathematics. Because of that, when I was very young, I started getting on the radar of people wanting to mentor me. That led to some great mentors, and in some cases, even filling a fatherly role.

I started my first legitimate business when I was nineteen, and I've continued to grow from there. One of my first mentors was one of the Forbes 400. He was number twenty-five on the list of the wealthiest people. Timing has a lot to do with success because he had lost a son who was about my age. I didn't really have that fatherly role, so we kind of filled that void for each other.

In the beginning, it started off as a mentor/ mentee relationship, and then we started to collaborate and partner. He knew all the celebrities and the most successful people on the planet and had billions of dollars, but what impressed me the most was his level of humility and his subservient leadership style.

If you were having dinner, he would hop up and say, "Are you done with this? Let me clear your plate for you. Let me fill your drink." He was always gracious and kind. You don't expect a person in that position to be that way, and I try to emulate him.

As part of my work, companies bring me in, have me sign an NDA, and then have me look at their books. Some of these are the largest companies in the world. I would find mathematical incongruences of where the business would fall apart.

Someone once told me, "You have a very special opportunity because you're working with the most successful people and companies on the planet. You're receiving a million-dollar education. So, you really need to pay attention to what you're learning and ask a lot of questions. However, I want to give you some advice."

"Knowledge," he said, "isn't experience. Experience is different. Although you're receiving this million-dollar education, you need to learn about people. You have to get into the people business. You have to learn sales." So, that's what I did.

I started several sales companies. I started selling door-to-door to learn the people side of things. Eventually, we got into franchises for medical equipment and other things, and did well, making around a million dollars a year. However, as I grew and learned from these other people, I learned that I was thinking small. I was capable of much more.

Now, I own a private equity fund with another Bellwether member. We invest in different commodities, oil, gas, other natural fuels, precious metals, real estate, crypto, and so on. We also advise. We advise a CEO who owns a sports team, we advise a few NFL players, and we advise a couple of other CEOs. We give them guidance and direction.

Years ago, I founded a book publishing company called Indigo River Publishing. We just happened to do things right, and it grew pretty big. We eventually became partners with Simon & Schuster. My old assistant is now the CEO of that publishing company.

What is interesting is how I first met him. At the time, I was in the seminar business. After one of my seminars, a young man came up to me and said, "Hey, I was at your seminar yesterday, and I wanted to shake your hand."

I was checking out of my hotel, so he, his girlfriend, and I started talking. He was about thirty years old and a sharp young guy.

I said, "Hey, do you live here in Orange County?" This was where I was doing the seminar. He said, "Actually, my girlfriend and I live in front of the hotel." I said, "What do you mean?" He said, "We live in our car."

Come to find out, he was a rockstar engineer in his twenties and worked for the largest tool company in the world. Then, they saw the movie *Into the Wild*, quit their jobs, and went off-grid. He knew there had to be more to life than sitting in a box.

A deal I've been making for about twenty years is, if I like the person and see potential, I say, "Look, give me a year to educate and mentor you. At the end of the year, I'll back you financially in anything you want to do. I'll be your backer, but you got to give me one year, and then we'll be partners in something." I made that deal with this young man.

I said, "By the way, at the end of the year, what do you want to do?" He said, "I didn't tell you before, but I'm a trained writer from the Institute of Children's Literature. I'd like to get into more writing and even publishing." Even though I didn't know anything about publishing, I said it sounded great, and we'd figure it out.

So that's how my book publishing came about, by honoring my deal. At the end of the year, I said, "Okay, you have to build some relationships with the big guys. There are six major billion-dollar publishing conglomerates, including Random House, McGraw-Hill, and Simon & Schuster. You have to find mentors. I'll keep the doors open, but we have to fail fast so we can figure this out."

Since I had contacts from the seminar business, I was able to sign a few people right away, but it was difficult. They thought it sounded amazing, but when they asked if I had a book I could show them, I had to say that we didn't have any yet; we were brand new.

Eventually, I got some speakers signed and some of the right people, but it was definitely like pushing a boulder up a steep hill. As we continued to grow our catalog into the hundreds, and I started signing, not only

some well-known entrepreneurs, but celebrities as well, it attracted Simon & Schuster. When they took over all of our distribution, and we formed a partnership, I took that as my exit strategy. I'm now more in an advisory kind of situation.

There are a few things people seem to always get wrong in business. Number one is they're focused on revenue. Most small business owners are trying to increase their numbers; they're trying to increase sales and revenue. What I've learned from great guidance, mentorship, and experience is that creating wealth, particularly generational wealth, has very little to do with revenue.

You could make $20 an hour and still be generationally wealthy in fewer than five years. It doesn't really have to do with your income, either. It has to do with taking on strategic debt and the accumulation of assets. You use other people's money, such as banks or other lenders. The middle-class chase revenue, which is a mistake. That's a long, "thirty-five years until retirement" kind of play.

Another mistake is when people do not take into consideration the way that math works. For a typical business at the end of the startup phase and getting into its rhythm, they're dealing with at least 1,500

variables. There are a lot of moving parts.

The first few decisions you make might include: Where are we going to be located? What product or service are we going to sell? What can we get it for? What can we sell it for? Who's going to be on our team? What's our domain? What are we going to call the business?

We tend to make those first eight decisions very quickly. The way we randomly put them together, unbeknownst to us, creates an inevitability. As time goes on, those variables we throw together will add, subtract, multiply, and divide in a particular pattern that results in a finite number. We don't know what that number will be, but if we could fast-forward in time, we would know if it's too little or enough.

People have an idea of how much is enough, so they start building a bridge from where their business is currently to the number they have in mind. They'll build business very linearly, such as: We're going to start with this many people. We're going to sell this product. We're going to do this thing. We're going to have a small location, with minimal fixed overhead, and so on. But they reach a point where there's a giant cliff between where they are and the number they want to reach because they have no more data.

We have the historical data, present data, which you may or may not have right now, and future data, which hasn't happened. This means they can only build linearly to a certain point because the cliff can only be crossed with future data that you don't have. There are two ways to get this data when you need it. You can either project or predict.

Most people will merely project. A pet peeve of mine is when they use speculation of future market share capture. As an investor myself, I get pitched on at least ten deals a week. They'll say, "Guys, it's a multi-billion-dollar industry. If we could just get 1% of 1%, it's this much money." They use very grandiose pitches, but they're just speculating about future markets or capture.

So, they'll build the bridge as far as they can to the cliff, and when they can't go any further, they'll go to the other side and build a bridge back using speculation of future markets for capture. They make it look like a cohesive plan. Meanwhile, they have no legitimate evidence or congruency in their math that it could work or that they even have a shot of getting that percentage of market share capture. It's not real.

If you want to fix this problem, you have to start with the end or goal in mind. You don't have to have the "how" of how you're going to build this giant business. You might only have five percent of the how. You don't have to have all the how, but you do have to have the first six or eight variables. Mathematics gives us a way that, even if I only have

a couple of variables, I can move those in different sequences until it tells me all the present data and even the future-based data. It'll even tell you where to be standing and when.

The only difference between projecting accurately, which a lot of companies do, and having the ability to predict, is the presence of enough math variables and a belief system. Huge companies like Siemens and Apple do not project quarters or where they will be at the end of the year in revenue, for example. Instead, they hire mathematicians to go from projecting to predicting. They actually know what the trend will be and what will happen. Math allows you to do that.

Success is not fully based on effort. You need to have a good work ethic, but it's not about your work ethic. It's not about how intelligent you are. It's not about grinding. It's math-based, and anybody can do it.

We groom about twenty people a year as a way of giving. For people who make $10 an hour, their business acumen, on a scale from one to ten, is a one. Within sixty months, we can make them not only millionaires, but quite wealthy if they follow the program. That is because it's just math based.

A lot of people look to people like Tony Robbins, Gary Vaynerchuk, or Grant Cardone, and they think that is the highest level of education. It's not. Those guys look to the Forbes 400, and they try to model after the Fortune 10 companies.

Math is so amazing because it allows us to do things that are almost superhuman. When I hire these young people to mentor them, I start by teaching them one skill while I give them three months of a paid apprentice program.

In the end, if they're doing good, I teach them one or two more skills so they're making a couple thousand dollars a month. Then, we have to get to eight to ten thousand dollars a month in their first year.

By the end of the second year, they're well into six figures. By the end of the third year, they're an asset-rich millionaire. And then at the end of four and five years, they're pretty serious people. With math, all of us can do that.

Today, The Bellwether Alliance is pretty much my full-time work. I spend most days speaking with Bellwether members around the world, trying to add value in any way I can.

Bellwether was around a long time before me, but I kind of took it over. Most of the elements of Bellwether came out of Spain in the late 1500s. I took over my current position as Viceroy about four years. At the time, it was more of a boy's club. It was always based on core values and ethics, but they would basically use the credo of Bellwether. They would come together and do deals on a handshake. It was where they could do honest joint ventures and trust each other.

There were no women, either. Over time, it grew into something that was really significant. This was well before the digital age, so they would assign handwritten record keepers. Over time, those records became fragments as people died. I was commissioned to put it back together in the modern age. I had to convince people that, just because we're private, it doesn't mean we can't have a website with at least a little information for the public.

A lot of these types of organizations start off as just a boy's club or a secret fraternity. But I knew The Bellwether Alliance needed to be a legal corporation. I feel like I had fragments of a box of dinosaur bones that I had to piece together to function in the modern world.

That was a pretty big job. I'm still putting some pieces together, but it took a few years to do that, even with the help of a very good team.

It's nice for Bellwether members to get some of the information. Outside of Bellwether, I want people to know that there is an organization that stands for good and that is truly focused on members and others. The members are people who have vowed to uphold a very high standard when it comes to morality, values, and ethics.

We have 52 success laws we call elevation laws that we abide by. Those teachings are really what the one-percenters have. The organization is very adamant about teaching every single member those laws.

A lot of members say things like, "Wow, with the value I'm getting at Bellwether, how come it's not $25,000 or $50,000 a year?" We've seen these high-end mastermind groups where it's very elitist, and only the wealthy can afford them. But becoming a member is absolutely closed to the public. No one can join unless somebody vouches for you.

It's never been about being wealthy. The prerequisite to getting into Bellwether is being a good person and how you treat others. It's living by the credo and being cut from a very high moral cloth, living a life of subservient leadership.

Now, the nature of the organization does attract a lot of very wealthy people, but it's never been elitist, where we exclude people who might be teachers, engineers, architects, or scientists. We don't want to take a bunch of rich people and teach them how to be good people. We want to take a bunch of good people, and if they're not already wealthy, teach them the principles they need to create generational wealth so they can garner the appropriate resources to expand their gift and expand their impact.

I want people to know that there is an organization that operates that way. But they do have to know someone in the organization who will give them the nod. If they continue to do good, people will notice, and at some point, someone in Bellwether will probably notice them.

We have to separate the difference between what we think is possible and what is probable. In my seminars, I talk about finding an actual probability rate.

As an investor, I don't care about what's possible because I think most things are possible. Instead, what is the probable outcome of a scenario? There's a way to calculate the probability. If somebody comes to me and wants my time or money or both, I have a very fixed metric of what the probable outcome is. If it's out of my range, I'm out. It's unemotional. I just look at the probable outcome of things.

If you're not getting the amount of success you feel you deserve, if you're not hitting the levels you think you're capable of, it might not be your fault. You might be behind the right product or service, the right company, the right team, or the right work ethic, but you've merely selected a few wrong variables. You might have 97% of the dots correctly connected with just a few dots left to connect. Finding the right mentor can help you do that.

For people in Bellwether who reach out to me, I help them try to connect those last few dots. I know that anybody can have generational wealth within five years or less.

DEAN WEGNER

When people say, "Dean, tell me about yourself," I say I'm a veteran, I'm an entrepreneur, and my priorities in life align with God, family, and country. I am passionate about making a difference. My Christian faith is first and foremost in my life, and family is just as incredibly important.

My wife, Kelly, and I will be celebrating twenty-eight years of marriage this month, and we also have four amazing kids. We have two daughters, twenty-four and twenty-one. We have an eighteen-year-old son, and we also have a twelve-year-old son we adopted from Ethiopia. He's been with us for ten years, and I could not imagine life without him. We're very blessed with such an amazing family.

I am a veteran, and I graduated from West Point in 1993. I went on to flight school and learned how to fly helicopters. I had a unique opportunity to see the aviation side of the Army. I went to Ranger school and served for seven years, and the incredible memories of the men and women I served with ultimately led to an intentional choice to donate ten percent of our profits to veteran and first-responder charities.

Authentically American is a veteran-owned, American-made, premium apparel brand. We have an amazing product, and it's all made right here in the US. To give you an idea of how rare that is, when I graduated from West Point in 1993, over fifty percent of the apparel was made in the US. Today, it's less than three percent. That shocking statistic gave birth to our tagline, "Where's yours made?"

The heart of our mission is our passion for creating American jobs. We have an amazing product that's all American-made. We want you to choose American-made when given a choice.

There are two sides to our business. There's the consumer side, the B2C side, which is primarily through our website, including some items that are Authentically American branded. We were back on national TV last week on *Fox and Friends*, and one of the bestsellers was our fun patriotic socks. They are Carolina cotton, knit in North Carolina. We have done hundreds of custom designs, and that's one example of the Authentically American brand.

What I'm wearing right now has the West Point logo. We also have collegiate licenses, along with the Naval Academy, Air Force Academy, VMI, Citadel—all the military schools. In Nashville, we've got great schools like Vanderbilt, Belmont, and MTSU. We recently added Alabama and Auburn, and we're getting ready to add Texas A&M.

That's the consumer side, but 80% of our business is B2B. Most businesses, charities, and organizations buy branded apparel that includes their company logo. And nothing, for the most part, is American-made.

I mentioned the *Fox and Friends* interview last week. For our fifth anniversary, *Forbes* magazine did a feature story on us, and they highlighted the work we're doing with some Fortune 500 companies, like

Pepsi, Comcast, Bridgestone, and Procter & Gamble, and also some big recognizable charities, like the Wounded Warrior Project, Tunnel to Towers Foundation, and Team Red White & Blue.

When I say I'm a veteran and an entrepreneur, I have to laugh because when I left the Army in 2000, I couldn't even spell entrepreneur. I didn't know this whole world existed. My dad was an engineer for Alcoa, a Fortune 100 aluminum company, for thirty years. Most of his friends and neighbors worked for big companies also, so when I left the Army in 2000, what did I think I was going to do? Work for a big company, of course.

I spent a couple of years with a Big 5 consulting firm, KPMG. I loved my clients, but I loved my family more, and I never saw them. I transitioned to Procter & Gamble, which is a phenomenal company, a world-class marketing and branding company, and I worked on brands like Crest and Tide. I also spent time at Mars, another world-class marketing and branding company, and had brands like M&M's, and Snickers, along with their pet food division. They're phenomenal companies, and Procter & Gamble is an $80 billion company. Mars is half the size but is still a $40 billion company.

I mentioned having an insatiable desire to make a difference. At one point, I realized that, although I had fairly large jobs and was very well paid, if you pulled me out, the next guy would step right up, and the machine wouldn't skip a beat. I truly wondered if I was making a difference if I was so easily replaced. That provided the motivation for me to become an entrepreneur.

One reason I left the Army was to stop moving. I wanted to plant roots and invest in a community. It's interesting because I moved even more after the Army. For example, during my six years with Procter and Gamble, I lived in four different cities. When we arrived in Nashville in 2010, it was move number ten.

My wife grew up in Tennessee. It's a great state to raise a family in, and I knew if we had to move one more time, I was probably going by myself. That led down the path of ultimately buying a business. I didn't think I had it in me to start a business from scratch, so I bought an existing business in 2012, a government contractor that produced dress uniforms for the military.

What was kind of neat was the old Army dress pants I used to wear were one of our contracts. We had thousands of uniforms we produced every week for the Army, Navy, Air Force, and Marines. I'm very passionate about creating jobs, and my initial thinking was that I wanted to win more contracts to create more jobs. But as a government contractor, if I won the bid for a job, those jobs simply transferred to my company from the previous company. New jobs weren't created. That's when the light bulb went off, and I thought, *What if, rather than being a government contractor, we built a brand instead?*

I thought back to the days when I worked for P&G and Mars, working on brands like Crest, Tide, and M&M. I thought, *What if, instead of doing what 97% of brands were doing and chasing cheap labor overseas, we made the intentional choice to produce right here in the US and only in the US? Think of the difference*

we could make and the jobs we could create. If we deliver on our vision to build this iconic American brand with the same recognition as Nike or Under Armour but all American-made, what an incredible legacy we could leave.

Our clothes are manufactured all across the US. Nike, for example, produces in China, Vietnam, Bangladesh, and all around the world, but they don't *own* those facilities. They contract with them. We have a contract facility in North Carolina outside of Raleigh that produces socks. Our collegiate t-shirts are produced in Texas. Our chambray dress shirts are made in California. Our clothes are produced in eleven states. I find the best manufacturers in the country so that I can focus on marketing, branding, and customer experience.

One stereotype we fight is the idea that, because we're American-made, we must be outrageously expensive. Fortunately, that's not true, and that is partially because of our choice of business model. We choose to sell direct only so we can remain competitive. Most brands follow the more common distributorship model, where there is a

wholesale layer that provides a substantial markup.

And this is across industries, but general studies out there would show that the average consumer is willing to pay a 12% premium. And there's a much larger gap for me to produce a t-shirt here in the US versus in China. There's one primary reason that we're able to be competitive, and that is a business model choice.

As an example, Southwest Airlines does this as well. If you want to fly Southwest, you can't buy your tickets on Travelocity or Expedia. You can only buy via southwest.com. Our model right now is all about buying direct. We cut out the middleman. Most people love our product. They love that we're American-made, they love the quality of our clothing, and they find a way to work with us.

If you're a new entrepreneur looking to build a business, find what you love. Find what you're passionate about, and it will make all the difference. I'm not shy about hard work. When I was an Army Ranger, I would often live on one meal a day and two to three hours of sleep for weeks in a row. But over the last five years, I have worked more than I ever have before. At one point, my wife was worried about my health, but she realized that when I wake up at 3:00 in the morning, long before the alarm goes off, it's because I love what I'm doing. I'm passionate about what I'm doing.

As hard as I'm working, it doesn't feel like hard work because I'm pursuing my passion. Let me tell you how that has played out. Our very first national TV appearance was in 2018 on *Fox and Friends*. We've now been on national TV, including *Fox and Friends, Fox Business News, Yahoo*, NASDAQ, and more.

In this digital age, it's relatively easy to communicate a story, but you must have a great product. You need to be competitively priced, but people want a little more. For example, we're a brand that celebrates patriotism. We believe in the American worker, and we're a brand that honors our American heroes. We donate ten percent of our profits to veteran and first-responder charities.

There are hundreds of charities we work with, including the Wounded Warrior Project, the Tunnel to Towers Foundation, and Team Red, White & Blue. We provide our goods and services at cost. We can't afford to give it away, but what we found that charities, especially veteran and first-responder-focused charities, love that we're American-made. They love that we're veteran-owned and when we're providing goods at cost, they not only have an opportunity to get amazing American-made products, but we help them build their brand and raise money in the process.

In addition to pursuing your passion and finding a cause, spend time investing in relationships. I was a hockey player at West Point and still play in a men's beer league now. I love sports. My kids were soccer players and hockey players, so we're a big sports family. I think business, even if you're a sole proprietor, is the ultimate team sport. You have to rely on your banker, your attorney, and your CPA, and I invest heavily in those business relationships.

It's never about what other people can do for me; it's what I can do for them. It's amazing when you have that mindset. People genuinely feel that you have their back and that you're willing to help. And miraculously, that comes back tenfold. I've found that people are willing to help me out because I help them. That's how our first national TV appearance came together. One of our suppliers ended up having a connection with *Fox and Friends*, sent them our story, and a month later, we were asked to be on the show.

JAMES ANDERSON

I'm somewhat of a country boy. I was born in Roanoke Rapids, North Carolina, but when I was very young, we moved to Chesapeake, Virginia. I am the oldest of three boys in my family, and I also have an older sister. My two younger brothers typically followed in my footsteps. My middle brother is only thirteen months younger than me, and we're close to each other.

I grew up just like most kids, playing sports and enjoying life. I had a great family, and my parents are still married. My mother is an educator, so school was always important to our family. My father is a minister, and together, they gave us a strong foundation of principles, ethics, and a belief system. I think that foundation supported me in my quest to become whatever I wanted to do. Whatever we approached with faith as one of the leading principles, we were always successful.

Growing up, my parents taught me a healthy balance of correction, but they also let me go out into the world a little, figure it out on my own, and come back with a bloody nose if necessary. Then they'd say, "Well, this is why we told you not to do that." But they knew I had to learn some lessons the hard way.

I learned that every action had a consequence, so I learned to avoid the actions that brought me negative responses and seek the actions that brought me positive consequences. Overall, I guess the biggest lesson I learned as a child growing up was how to filter my consequences that way and then how to use that to make better decisions.

Another big lesson I learned was to always do right by people. It is important to take care of people and be intentional about what you put out, whether the energy or the action, whether giving or receiving. You treat people a certain way, and people give that to you in return. Those are two big lessons that I try to live my life by.

I was always an honor student. If I brought home a C grade, I would be in trouble. Education has always been important to me, and not only because of how I was raised. No matter how much money you make or what you acquire, all of that can be taken from you. However, nobody can take what you learn and experience. That's why education has always been important to me.

I got cut from football every year until I started high school, so who would've ever imagined that I'd make it to the NFL. I ended up going to college at Virginia Tech. I went there initially for engineering and ended up going into graphic design guy and getting a degree in art. I stayed a fifth year in school because my football dreams hadn't formalized yet, and I ended up getting my master's in education. I was then blessed and fortunate enough to get drafted in the third round by the Carolina Panthers.

I lived my NFL dream and experienced all the ups and downs, the pressures, the ins and outs, from the outhouse to the penthouse, back to the outhouse, and then in the backyard. I went through that whole process and was blessed to play for ten years, which is pretty good in the NFL. That journey led me to where I am now: a father of two beautiful girls, trying to do what I can to be an example of what a man is supposed to be.

My parents were very supportive, strong people, and I try to be a good father as well. I have a lot of respect for my father. We never really butted heads, mostly because he's 6' 2" and 240 pounds. He's bigger than me, so there isn't really much head-butting. He's a man of few words, and when he spoke, we listened. It was either that or experience his forearm to your chest.

I suffer from a complex that is common with most people who have been successful. It's called perfectionism. I would rather not do anything for fear of being wrong. I dislike making mistakes and being wrong. But that was the lesson I learned during my first couple of years in the NFL: You can't always be right. I tried to study every play and look at every outcome and try to predict every play as they would come in formation. I had it down to a science.

During my first couple of years in the league, my progress was slower than I anticipated because I tried to know everything. When it came down to a formation, for example, I thought I needed to know all of the possible plays. I felt I had to know everyone who was going to be in the game. Everything. And while I was thinking about all that, they're snapping the ball, and now I'm two steps too late.

Everybody who goes into professional sports gets something different out of it. They come out of the experience with their own set of lessons learned. What I learned or received from being in professional sports is not easy to answer because my journey has never been typical.

I remember when I was a rookie and was unhappy about my performance after a certain game. When Monday morning came, I just knew the coach was about to rip me a new one. But there was an older linebacker, Dan Morgan, sitting next to me. He said, "Bro, don't beat yourself up. They're going to do it for you. Remember that nothing is as good as it seems and nothing is as bad as it seems, so just take it how it comes."

I learned that lesson. Throughout my career and throughout life, I realized it was all about perspective. It's how you show up that makes the difference.

That kept me more levelheaded as I approached game study or film. I never got too high or too low; I stayed even-keeled. You celebrate the good games, and obviously, you never want to lose, you never want to have a bad game, but that perspective kept me from getting too low. Some days there were people in the spotlight who I had helped to get there, while other days, I was in the spotlight but only because other people helped me get there. Neither the celebration nor the disappointment was ever solely on my shoulders.

As I have moved on from my professional football career, there are three distinct areas in my life I am passionate about. The first is being a father. I have structured my life in such a way that I can be present as a father. I've turned down jobs and made specific decisions so I'm always able to control my time.

I can fix breakfast for my daughter, I can walk her to school, and I can be at the PTA meetings because I still have control over my time. Being a father and husband goes hand-in-hand and is most important to me.

MAKE A DIFFERENCE

The second big passion of mine is the work I'm doing with a friend of mine. We're developing a school called the Conscience Institute. The principles of the school go along with mindfulness, emotional intelligence, teaching kids by making use of their learning styles, as well as giving them real-world skills. It's not the typical curriculum you'd find in a school environment, although it is school. And along with that, we're developing a program called International Dad.

We are putting together resources and tools for men, not only to be present and available, but to have emotional intelligence, learn conflict resolution, and learn how to deal with the trauma of their life so they don't pass it on to their kids. I feel the best way to help shape the trajectory of the next generation is to influence the people who are influencing them. If we can create a safe environment for emotional growth, as well as help fathers and men to be present, then we can change the next generation for the better.

The third passion is more personal, and that's pursuing another sport—long drive. As a professional athlete, for my mental well-being, there has to be a competitive aspect in my life. A lot of people go into coaching or sales because it's always about the competition. I feel that having that extra competitive edge is what has allowed people like me to achieve high success in professional athletics.

For me, right now, that's venturing into long drive. I'm still an amateur, but I'm teetering on turning pro because that gives me a new arena in which to compete as well as something I feel I can be one of the best in the world at. It gives me another opportunity to be a part of that one percent.

A fourth passion is working with a self-creative agency where we do tech as well as creative work for other projects. That agency has allowed me to work with AI, plus we do weapons detection work that helps school systems. It's all about empowering and providing safety for generations to come.

I had a mentor growing up, and he always told me, "Every person who comes to this life has two things in common: They were born on this day, and they died on this day. Every single person has those two things in common. The only difference is the dash in the middle. What do you want to do with your life? What impact do you want to make? When James Anderson goes away from this world, what's left behind? How many people did you impact? What difference did you make?"

Everything I do—whether it's the intentional dad program, the self-creative agency, the Conscience Institute, or even long drive—is for that purpose. If I made a difference in this world, if I made a positive impact on people's lives, then I've done my job.

JOY VANICHKUL

From modeling, entrepreneurship, yoga training, and pursuing a Ph.D. in natural sciences to sharing inner peace practices, there is an innate hunger in me to learn and improve every day. All of my endeavors reflect this drive.

My modeling career exposed me to many cultures as I traveled the world. It eventually led me along another path—entrepreneurship—when I founded the Zense of Joy Spa.

I opened Zense of Joy Spa to create a comprehensive haven that blends inner beauty with outer beauty. I added a medical spa center and a beauty product line to diversify my business. I used social media to spread the message, and my slimming product range became a huge success.

I established a chain of spas where I combined the magic of Thai herbs with the world's best spa techniques. My spa enterprise soon grew into a multi-million-dollar business. My level-headed leadership and dedicated team of 200 people earned my business a nomination for Best New Spa.

When I came to the United States, I decided to attend a yoga school. My intention was never to teach. I just wanted to learn. But I promised my yoga teacher that I would impart my learning to others, and I am keeping that promise.

I'm a certified hypnotherapist, a 500 RYT yoga instructor, a certified children's yoga teacher, a meditation instructor from the Middle Way Meditation Institute, a Heart-Math Institute certified trainer, and a Ph.D. scholar in Natural Medicine. Additionally, I study and train in health, nutrition, neuroscience, and quantum physics, among other subjects.

My only focus now is to see what I can bring to the community and contribute to making this a better place. I want to be able to teach other women. I've learned a lot, and I want to contribute to others now.

I provide one-on-one mentorship and consultations that can last anywhere between one and six months. My co-founded program, Inner Peace Life Education, a meditation and yoga program at Tree Academy, a private middle and high school in Los Angeles, is something I'm proud of. I have seen students report less stress, have increased concentration ability, and reconnect peacefully with themselves.

I practice meditation religiously. I grew up in Bangkok, Thailand, watching my mother and grandmother practice meditation every day. It was a strong influence in my life and made it better.

I founded many meditation programs that are aimed at helping people discover the truth of reality and understand their potential. I've also traveled to distinct parts of the world to host peace events. World Peace, through Inner Peace, gathered over 100,000 people, and the Light of Peace event was acknowledged by the United Nations for bringing many spiritual leaders together to bring peace to the world.

I've been launching specific wellness programs for women, one of which is Intelligent Beauty. This program is specifically aimed at women leaders to regain their power through consciousness.

I became aware of the pattern of how people perceive beauty and realized I could help bridge the gap by creating a collective awareness of the true meaning of beauty. The Intelligent Beauty Method was designed to be a precious commodity containing my extensive knowledge of ancient eastern and western spiritual practices and 30 years of experience building my foundation of success by upholding the three pillars of Intelligent Beauty as a wellness entrepreneur, consciousness teacher, and a connoisseur of beauty. Now everyone can embody Intelligent Beauty and receive high-value tools and techniques they can apply immediately to obtain life-changing results.

Intelligent beauty (IB) is a state of harmony between internal and external beauty qualities while optimizing productivity and creativity. Intelligent Beauty emerges from the heart's qualities and values, love, courage, and compassion. It positively affects one's perceptions, attitudes, and beliefs toward the true virtue of beauty. This

The Intelligent Beauty Method (IBM) is a methodology built upon three pillars: Wellness, Beauty, and Consciousness.

Society tells us that intelligence is the ability to learn, understand, or deal with new or trying situations. It combines cognitive skills and knowledge made clear through one's behaviors. But there's so much more to it. Intelligence is the combination of cognitive skills and knowledge collected from life's experiences that branches out from the ability to learn, understand, or manage one's thoughts, emotions, and actions, as well as to connect one's consciousness to reach a higher level of awareness and intuition.

Beauty is energy and expanded consciousness. True beauty starts from within by cultivating the qualities and values of the heart: love, kindness, compassion, peace, authenticity, integrity, courage, confidence, creativity, and intellect.

Beauty is a timeless power, a strength that holds compassion, kindness, elegance, and grace. At its core, beauty serves a purpose to better physical, emotional, spiritual, environmental, cultural, and mental well-being,

which in turn attracts love, prosperity, and abundance.

Society's definition of beauty is related to how attractive a person is based on their face and body characteristics, such as shape and symmetry. Those perceptions may change depending on the individual, society, and/or time period.

Modern societal standards are based on various forms of media (magazines, movies, commercials, online social platforms, etc.). The bar is set unrealistically high for women because of the constant push to look a certain way. Beauty is mainly perceived from external features, such as long legs, great hair, curves in the right places, perfect skin, flattering weight size, and trendy clothes.

The Intelligent Beauty Method helps liberate women from the misperceived definition of beauty. Women worldwide share the common burden of non-alignment with societal beauty standards, often leading to negative self-talk, self-doubt, poor self-image, low confidence, and so much more. Intelligent Beauty seeks to address these widespread issues for those who fall short of idealistic standards, left to feel inadequate and awkward, and those who fit the mold, often hiding their beauty out of fear that their physical attributes will overshadow their value and true self-worth.

Most people face challenges when accepting their beauty because the value of beauty is limited to societal misperception, focusing only on external beauty. True beauty is not only skin-deep. It penetrates deep down into the core of our being and creates well-being and balance. The absence of awareness of beauty creates unhealthiness and leads to confusion, misery, and suffering.

Everyone wants to feel beautiful, comfortable in their own skin and seen for who they truly are. One of the biggest challenges is that people don't understand the true benefit of beauty. They fall into the fault of fear because they want to be taken seriously and to prove their self-worth. Another challenge is a lack of confidence, which leads to a weak self-image that is not strong enough to withstand the spotlight. Instead of allowing themselves to shine brightly, they dim their light by sabotaging themselves to avoid attention. Self-destructive behavior may take the form of binge eating, overuse of alcohol, procrastination, depression, aggression, and loneliness.

The IB Method will guide women to have a profound, high-level impact on success, happiness, and fulfillment in their personal and professional lives. It will help women to awaken a power they never knew existed with a transformative, proven process no one has taught before. During and after this program, participants will see their essence of Wellness, Beauty, and Consciousness converted from the inside out for life fulfillment, satisfaction, and success.

The IB Method gives people the power to liberate themselves from outer perceptions of what beauty is supposed to be. They will understand clearly that there are many choices and successfully create their own version of beauty. People will gain extensive knowledge on cultivating and leveraging their inner and outer beauty through the proven IBM curated by top experts across the globe in the beauty, wellness, and spiritual world.

Immediately participants receive a fresh new perspective and continue discovery throughout the program and long after. The time to results is based on each individual's dedication to establishing the new baseline which transforms their life, moving beyond limitations towards their ultimate goals.

The purity of beauty starts at the center of your heart. External beauty gives your heart a voice to be seen and understood. It uplifts and empowers the individual, leading to self-respect, confidence, and success. With an impenetrable armor crafted from the knowledge of great skincare, flawless makeup, and an elegant style tailored to each unique individual, no one can deny the beauty that resides within. External beauty gives those who know how to wield its shield the persuasive power to conquer their desires.

Intelligent Beauty Method provides well-rounded, holistic support by offering:

- Comprehensive information on optimizing a healthy lifestyle
- Cutting-edge tools and techniques
- Simple, practical steps to follow
- Direct knowledge from the leading experts in the beauty, wellness, and consciousness communities
- A collaborative community for support
- Intelligent energy management
- Wellness group
- Live meditation, meditation circles
- Online course
- Beauty and well-being retreats
- Workshop
- Seminars

- Access to resources through monthly subscriptions
- Group coaching with Joy
- Wellness products
- Beauty products
- Expanded consciousness products
- Meditation and affirmation recordings
- Private channel of social communication

Pick the right business that synchronizes with your heart and brain. It's important to choose what your heart says to follow and where your intelligence fits in. Once you choose an area where your calling is, you will be inspired to go to the workplace and deliver your best rather than just dragging there.

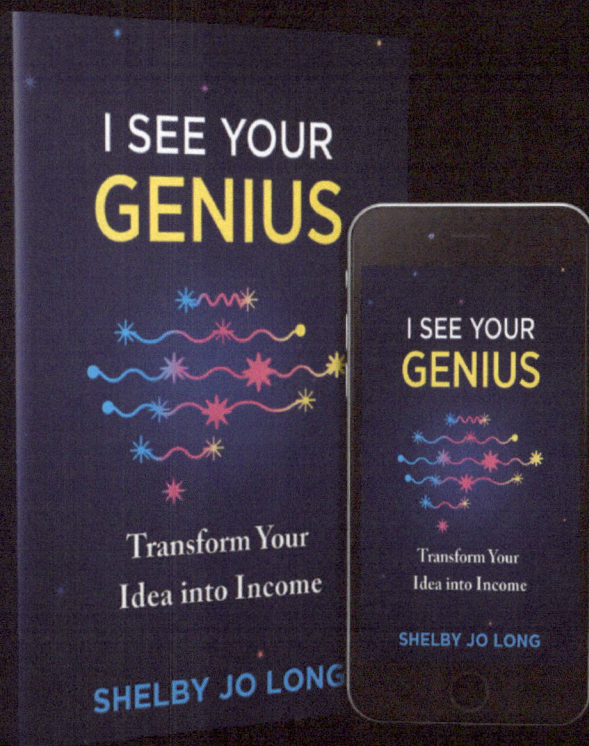

MORRY DAVID

I've been an entrepreneur all my life and found that many entrepreneurs tend to micromanage and do many things themselves. They feel they are the only person best suited for whatever their vision is, and only their driving passion can help them accomplish their goals. I fell into that category.

I've had many successful businesses, but I quickly recognized that I had to change my modus operandi if I wanted to go to the next level. So that's what I did. Although I was proud of my achievements, I had to change my mindset to accomplish even greater things.

This caused me to pivot, which has allowed me to do what I could never do before.

I realized that scaling my businesses would require more of my time and not necessarily yield proportional profits. Did I really want to put in those hours?

I turned the question around and asked myself, *Could my businesses actually run with me working fewer hours instead of more? Could I give myself time to pursue something that would be even greater than my businesses?*

The first thing I did was to progressively work fewer hours to determine how much of my time was actually needed to maintain my businesses. I got it down to 20%, which freed up 80% of my time.

Next, I asked myself if I just wanted to watch television and go on vacation or could that time be used in areas that were more beneficial. To do something greater, should I follow the same pathways used to create my businesses, or should I accept the challenge of designing a better way?

I realized that micromanaging and trying to do everything on my own was my greatest fault. Even though I had employees, I actually slowed their progress by jumping into everything.

I was lucky to find and join an organization that had a tremendous number of very talented and nice people. And as I got to know these people, I realized that they had the same problems as me.

I found myself standing outside their box and giving them advice, and they reciprocated by standing outside my box. And lo and behold, we found we had common goals. We all wanted to move to the next level, and as a team, we could accomplish incredible things.

That was a major pivot point in my understanding of how businesses should work. All of a sudden, I had a team, a very special team that changed my life.

I started to pivot about five years ago. One of the first things I did to flame my passions was to start writing. It was something I was always capable of doing; I just never had the time. My first book quickly became a bestseller in three hours, and my second book

became a bestseller immediately upon its release.

I examined the publishing industry and my expectations. I soon realized that I could not generate a substantial income selling books. My biggest problem was that I lacked the audience of popular writers like Stephen King. I didn't have 20,000 people who would immediately buy my books. Even with my background in marketing, I'd have to work extremely hard to sell tens of thousands of books.

I realized there were other opportunities to make a great deal of money from my stories rather than selling one book at a time. I looked at the entertainment industry, such as Netflix, Amazon, and other streaming services that were booming. They had their own projects and were making their own movies. Their problem was a lack of content. They didn't have enough writers. So, I thought: *is this the best way of doing it? Why don't I just take one of my books and create a mini-series for Amazon?*

I was heading in that direction when I was given advice by my publisher and dear

friend. He said, "Yes, that's an idea, but what you just wrote is much bigger than a mini-series. You shouldn't give it to Amazon. The amount of money you'll receive is certainly more than you would get just selling books, but it is not nearly what it is worth. You wrote the equivalent of a major motion picture, and you should pursue that."

My problem was that I didn't know people in the movie industry. I once again reached out to my organization and asked for help and was pleasantly surprised at the response.

I was shown that it's not what you know but who you know, how you get your passions known, how you ignite other people's passions, and how you build a team. When that happens, the magic begins.

That was a major pivot point in my life. I moved from running my businesses to being a writer and entering the movie business. Although I am now a producer with limited field knowledge, I have people behind me helping me every step of the way. I feel lucky and have learned to set my ego aside and accept help.

Everyone's passions are different. I have a strong entrepreneurial spirit, and because of my education in marketing, advertising, journalism, and electronics, I'm made from a different mold. What happens to me won't necessarily happen to someone else, but I always mentor others by saying: "Find your passion and go for it."

What you love isn't necessarily what you're doing for a living. In fact, sometimes, what you're doing for a living may be just surviving. You may not even realize that you are

in a box. You might have a large box with a nice home and nice cars, but you've become a slave to your own business.

My best advice for entrepreneurs is to always pursue your passions. What is the worst that could happen? If it doesn't work out, you don't lose anything. You didn't destroy what you previously had. You didn't sell off your businesses and spend $3 million going after something. You found ways of allocating your time and pursuing your passion. Many people want to see you succeed if they believe in you, but first, you have to believe in yourself.

I'm treading in uncharted territory, and this is a major pivot in my life. The first pivot was becoming a writer and recognizing my businesses could stand alone without me putting a lot of time in.

My second pivot was realizing that, as a writer, I could take it to the next level, which I did in the entertainment industry. What I'm doing in the movie industry is blending entertainment with education. It's been interesting to find that most movies don't have elements of education; they are strictly entertainment.

I looked at people like Walt Disney, and I thought, *He has done a wonderful job. His passions were ignited so much that, even though he hasn't been alive for a long time, they continue on all around the world. It's wonderful what he has accomplished, but it's for entertainment.*

Now, what happens if entertainment and education can be merged? For example, look at *Sesame Street*. It was a remarkable breakthrough because they both entertained and educated at the same time. How can I do this on a large scale and even make major changes in education, similar to what was done with *Sesame Street*? How can I take full advantage of technology? Children are on their notebooks, tablets, and phones. Why can't I blend all the technologies together and see what happens? That's my next pivot.

I've learned that you're only on this earth for a certain number of years, and nobody knows how long that will be. You can spend your life merely surviving, and many people do just that. However, what turns me on is asking myself what I can do in my life to make my grandchildren and great-grand-children say, "Hey, my grandfather did that!" Just like people still know the name: Walt Disney.

I'm not doing this for myself. I'm doing this to show people that anything can be done if you ignite your passions, align with the proper people, and educate yourself. If you believe in yourself, you can do anything. You can pivot out of any situation and move on, but you first have to believe it's possible. I think most people get so worn down in life that they just don't believe it and then don't try. And it's a shame.

If what I do inspires people, then that's great. Maybe they'll be inspired to really pursue their own passions instead of merely think-ing about them. I just finished my fourth book titled: *Why Some People Can Fly*. In it, I explain the processes of how society keeps us grounded. It's my goal to teach people how to leave their boxes and learn to fly and pivot!

THE REAL JASON DUNCAN

Entrepreneurs deal with something I call the hero syndrome, and that is when the entrepreneur puts on the cape, shows up, solves the problems, and saves the day. That is acceptable and even encouraged within the first few weeks to months of a startup. The problem is that the hero syndrome ends up sticking with entrepreneurs much longer than it should, and they sometimes wear the cape permanently. The business ends up revolving around them and their ability to solve problems and do things, and they don't learn to delegate. They don't give other people the opportunity to do what needs to be done on a regular basis.

Delegation is the act of assigning, entrusting, and empowering a person to act on your behalf. The only way to solve the hero syndrome is through delegation. The million and trillion-dollar companies we read about today in the news don't have a founder who still has hero syndrome. They have moved beyond that. They've learned to delegate. They've learned to offload tasks to other people.

Delegation is seen by most people as simply assigning a task, "Hey, Bob, I need you to go do this...," but that's only assigning, that's not delegating. Delegating is those three things I mentioned earlier—assigning, entrusting, and empowering. It moves beyond just assigning a task. It's also entrusting that task and empowering that person to do the task on your behalf. Therefore, when you say to Bob, "Hey, I need you to do something," you are assigning it, entrusting it, and empowering him to do it.

How do you do that?

First, Bob must know why the task has to be done, and not in the same way that you would answer a five-year-old who asks why about everything. Where does this task fit in the overall business and the company? Too often, employees think they're getting assigned a task simply because the boss doesn't want to do it. We have to make sure they understand why it needs to be done in the first place.

Second, they need to understand how to do the task, and sometimes that requires very specific instructions. Other times, it's as simple as telling them what needs to be done, why it needs to be done, and having the resources they need at their disposal.

To empower and entrust somebody to do that task, they need to know when it's due. Simply assigning them without going through the why, how, and when is only assigning a task and not delegating. Assign, entrust, empower. To do that, they've got to know why, they've got to know how, and they've got to know when.

What does delegation do for you? It gives you time, and time is the most important commodity that any entrepreneur could hope for. It's finite. You can't get it back. It's a non-renewable resource. Once time is spent, it's never coming back.

There was a study done by a lady named Gail Thomas in a book she released in 2013 called *The Gift of Time*. She revealed that 53% of business owners believe they can grow their business by more than 20% if they delegated 10% of their workload to somebody else. She went on to say that time is the biggest barrier to delegation, yet ironically, delegation saves us time.

The reason people don't delegate is they think it's going to take more time to give Bob a task and explain the why, how, and when than it would be to just do it themselves. The reality is you can do it faster and better than Bob, but you will always have to do it if Bob doesn't know how to do it. It would be better to invest the time now with Bob and get your time back later.

Gail Thomas's study went on to say that more than a third of business owners admit they should delegate more, and two-thirds recognize the value of it, but most people don't really know what delegation is. They think it's just assigning a task, and then they get frustrated because the other person doesn't do it the way they do it. There will be a dip in productivity, dip in outcome, dip in everything, but you will survive it if you commit to delegating. What you get in return is time.

What most entrepreneurs practice is not delegation. Instead, they either practice confiscation or abdication. It's like a pendulum, and one side of the pendulum is confiscation. Confiscation is when you pull something back and you take a task from its holder. In other words, you relinquish the task, and then you pull it back based on your authority to do the task to begin with. That's not delegation.

Confiscation never gets you back time. And what it looks like is this: "Hey Bob, I need you to do this task for me. Here's why, here's how, and here's when." Bob starts doing the task the right way, but what ends up happening is you look over Bob's shoulder, and you say things like, "No, it would be better if you did it this way. Just let me do it." You confiscate that task back, and then you've wasted time when you should have been out doing other tasks and being more productive. You've wasted Bob's and everybody's time.

That type of delegation leads to something called self-sabotage. Bob and all of your other employees will know that this is how you delegate; you confiscate. They even start thinking, *When he gives me a task I don't want to do, I'll screw up just enough that he'll take it back, and I don't ever have to do it.* It's like a husband who breaks enough dishes to where the wife will never ask him to wash dishes again. This hurts them. It hurts you. It hurts the business. True delegation is not confiscation.

The other side of the pendulum is abdication. Abdication is when you formally separate or divest yourself from the responsibility of the task. It's like relinquishing the throne. It's rightfully yours, but you relinquish it and never look back.

What that looks like is: "Hey, Bob, I need you to do this task. Here's why, here's how, and here's when." Again, you're starting the right way, but then as soon as Bob gives you the thumbs up, you turn around and walk in a different direction and never check in on

Bob. You don't know if Bob did or didn't do it. You don't know how bad it is until it's really bad. Sometimes abdication works because you have an A player you delegate to, and they do an amazing job.

But we all know that doesn't happen very often. Most of the time, you give it to Bob, and Bob is ignorant to what his real role is and doesn't execute it well. It causes more problems because you're not checking in to make sure he did it the right way. That's abdication. You can only emancipate yourself from the prison of the hero syndrome if you learn to truly delegate and neither confiscate nor abdicate.

Explaining the why, the how, and the when is important. And then there's a way to make sure that you don't confiscate and abdicate. Everything I've explained so far is the theory and the reality of what delegation is, what it is not, and how technically it's supposed to be done. But I put together a six-step process for entrepreneurs who want to learn to delegate so that they can actually practice delegation.

The first thing you're going to do is make a list of the top ten actions or activities you do on a regular basis that could be done by someone else, but that you're currently doing. You have to be honest. Maybe they're not going to be any

good at it, but they might be. So, make that top ten list.

The second thing is to pick one, and only one of those items, and delegate it to someone for thirty days. You limit your time. You go to Bob and say, "Bob, I have this one task I need to delegate this to you. Here's why, here's how, and here's when. It's only for thirty days. You good?" Bob knows it's only for thirty days. You know it's only for thirty days. You're learning how to delegate.

The third step, and this is where it starts getting hard, is you only check on their progress once a week—no more, no less. Something special happens when you do this. Bob knows you won't check in until Thursday at nine o'clock (or whatever time you've designated). You don't confiscate it back. You don't look over his shoulder every day, telling him to do it this way or that way. If you only check in once a week rather than a hundred times a week, you decrease the risk of confiscation.

The other side of that is, if you check in less than once a week, like if you just say, "Hey, get back to me in thirty days," you run the risk of abdication. Checking in once a week prevents the swinging back and forth of the pendulum. It becomes, "Hey, Bob, here's that task. Here's what you have to do.

We'll check in on Thursdays." And then you let Bob get out there and do it.

The fourth step is the hardest for everybody. It's looking for ways to praise their work without correcting them. This is a psychological issue. During your weekly check-in, Bob comes in and you say, "Hey, Bob, how have things been going?"

Whether Bob is doing great or he's a train wreck, you praise him. "Hey, I'm really glad you started doing it this way. That's actually a really good idea."

If it's a complete train wreck and everything's on fire, you look at Bob and say, "Well, I really like your tie today." You cannot correct them because if you correct them, they will rely on the hero to save them every single time. Employees will do that. It's natural. It's built into who we are, so don't correct them.

Now the caveat to this is, if Bob says directly, "Jason, I've been doing it this way, but I'm thinking about doing it this other way. Do you think that's a better way to do it?" Obviously, answer direct questions. "Yes. That'd be a better way to do it. Why do you think you should do it that way?" Teach and train, but don't critique when he comes in and says, "This is what I did. I think I'm doing fantastic." Don't look at it and say, "Oh, that's terrible. You can't do that." He must learn on his own.

We learn through failure. Failure is a greater teacher than success. As Bob fails through the process, he'll figure out better ways to do it. Remember, you didn't know how to do it as good as you do today when you first started. Bob doesn't either.

One more caveat: If somebody is in real danger or something catastrophically bad will happen, step in, correct them, and figure it out. But otherwise, if that's not going to happen, let them learn. You must coach them through this. You must step back. Let them figure out the answers.

Step one, make the top ten list.

Step two, pick one from the list, and delegate it for thirty days.

Step three, check in once a week—no more, no less.

Step four, you can only praise; you can't correct.

Step five is where it really starts to work. Once Bob can do the task at eighty percent of your ability to do it, it is never on your to-do list ever again. It is now permanently Bob's job, not yours, because you've proven that somebody can do it at eighty percent of your output.

Eighty percent is an important number because you can't look for perfection. You're not looking for somebody to be able to do it one hundred percent. That's not reality. Eventually, they're going to do it better than what you could do, but today you're only looking for eighty percent. Some people would argue that you could do fifty percent or sixty percent. I think eighty percent is the sweet spot.

Step six is to repeat that process every thirty days until your task list is either empty or only has one thing on it. The way this works is by repeating these things over and over again. Once you get the hang of it, you could assign four things at once or maybe even more. You might say, "Hey, I'm going to delegate eighteen things at once."

Once you get the hang of it and you're only checking in once a week, you're praising and not correcting, you're looking for that eighty percent success rate, you will be fine, and you can survive the dip.

There you have it, an easy-to-follow, six-step process. If you walk through that—whether you're an entrepreneur, a church leader, a business leader, or a parent—those six steps will make you a master delegator.

I hired a new assistant about two months ago. She was obviously a brand-new assistant and didn't know what we do or how we do it. Slowly, over the last two months, I've delegated more tasks to her. I've watched her grow in her ability to do things because I'm not confiscating.

For example, when I say, "Hey, I need you to get this new live webinar scheduled" and then I go into the Google sheet the next day, and it's not updated yet, even though I've written a standard operating procedure on how to do that, I don't freak out; I wait until we meet next Monday.

We meet the next Monday, and we go over everything she's been doing. I say, "Hey, by the way, this is not put in there. Is there a problem with the standard operating procedure that you've noticed that I didn't know about?"

She says, "You know what? I didn't follow the procedure. You're right."

So, it provides an opportunity for her to admit that she didn't do it and take responsibility by doing it. I could just go in and fill it in for her or specifically tell her to take care of it rather than having a conversation and empowering her to get it done.

Now, delegation is pretty natural for me. My time is more valuable to me than anything else. The more I can offload things, the

better. I was the entrepreneur hero for eight years in the business I started back in 2010. Everything revolved around me. I built good teams and had great people, but I still wore the cape every day. I was the guy who could save the day. Because of that, it robbed me of all the extra time I could have had.

Once I learned how to do this, I walked away from the daily operations of that business. I went on to start five other companies, including a coaching company. I was on a TED Talk international stage. I was only able to do that because I failed so long at it, and I decided that I didn't ever want to do that again. I studied delegation deeply so I could figure out how to step into the reality of the life I really wanted, which is being able to spend my time as I please, not as others require of me.

If you don't delegate, you're losing time. You're giving up time. At the end of your life, you're not going to wish you had done those reports yourself; you're going to wish other people had done more for you so you had more time.

Money is a renewable resource. Money, once spent, can come back. If I give someone $100 today, out of the goodness of my heart, I'm not worried about that $100 because I can make more money. But if I give someone 30 minutes of my time, I can't get that 30 minutes back. Most entrepreneurs leverage time to get money when I believe they should be leveraging money to get time.

ADVERTISERS